CAMBRIDGE ASSIGNMENTS IN MUSIC

Score-reading

ROY BENNETT

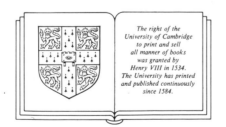

The right of the
University of Cambridge
to print and sell
all manner of books
was granted by
Henry VIII in 1534.
The University has printed
and published continuously
since 1584.

CAMBRIDGE UNIVERSITY PRESS
CAMBRIDGE
NEW YORK   NEW ROCHELLE
MELBOURNE   SYDNEY

Contents

* indicates score is included
  on transparencies

2

1
Scores and score-reading

'Score' comes from an Old English word *scoru*, meaning 'marked with scratches or lines'. It was first used by musicians to describe the way vertical lines were marked or scratched with a pen down through the staves of music to make *bar-lines* dividing, or measuring off, the music into separate *bars*. Later on, **score** came to mean a complete copy of a piece of music – either in manuscript (handwritten), or in print – with the parts arranged on separate staves, one above another, and linked by bar-lines so that the whole can be taken in at a glance.

The beginning of a composer's manuscript score and the printed score of the same music, showing: (a) name of the instrument which plays each part, (b) clefs, (c) key signature, (d) time signature, and (e) four staves of music linked together by (f) bar-lines.

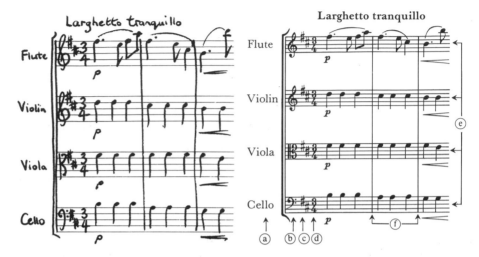

Types of score

There are various kinds and sizes of score. The most important include:

full score, showing the staves of music for all the instruments and/or voices taking part in a composition, and printed on large-size paper for easy reading (for example, by the conductor during performance);

miniature score (or **pocket score**), giving all the information shown in a full score but printed in a smaller size (about 13.5 cm by 19 cm) making it suitable for studying at home or taking to a concert;

vocal score, showing all the vocal parts of an opera or other work for voices and orchestra, but with the orchestral parts reduced to a two-stave arrangement which can be played on a piano.

Score-reading

In a strict sense, **score-reading** means taking a score to the piano and reproducing all the notes in every possible detail. Or even reading the notes from a score and hearing every one in your head, without any actually being sounded. However, musicians also use the term score-reading to mean *following* a score – that is, taking note of certain information given in the score, and following, or 'keeping up with', the music as it is being performed. And this, of course, is very much easier.

You will almost certainly find that following the score as the music is played will add to your enjoyment of a piece, and also help you to notice much more of the interesting detail in the music. Think of the score as a 'map', charting the course of the music. Your eyes will take in certain details and alert your ears; sometimes, it will be the other way around. Score-reading in fact involves close co-ordination of eye and ear, relating the look of information on the page to the sounds you hear – matching what you *see* to what you *hear*. So when following a score the rule is – *always use your eyes and ears to help each other.*

2
Following a melody-line score

In score-reading, the two most important aspects of the music, which help you to relate what you see to what you hear, are **pitch** and **rhythm**. The **pitch** of a note refers to how high or how low it sounds. The higher a note's position on the five-line stave, the higher it sounds. The kind of **clef** used indicates the general *range* of pitch – high, or low – you can expect to hear (see chart 2, page 92). You will not need to determine the pitch of any note precisely – this will be taken care of for you, of course, as the music is played. But it is important that you take account of the general 'contour' of the music – noting when it rises in pitch, falls in pitch, or (when notes are immediately repeated) remains at the same pitch.

Always *prepare* your listening by carefully looking through the score before the music is played. Refer to the charts and tables at the end of this book to discover the meaning of any points which may be new to you.

Look at the melody-line score below. First, notice the tempo (speed) marking in Italian (see chart 11, page 96). This gives an idea of how quickly your eye will need to travel to keep up with the music. This melody moves quite quickly – but there are many wide leaps for eye and ear to latch onto, and to help you check that you are keeping your place.

Note the time signature – four crotchet beats to each bar. As you listen, sense the strong first beat of each bar. Each of these is made very clear in this piece by a firm chord in the piano accompaniment.

The violin melody moves in even crotchets (the two notes in small type at bar 13 are 'grace notes', played lightly just before the beat). Notice that bars 3 and 4 are repeated exactly to become bars 5 and 6. and that bars 7–8 and 9–10 form a *sequence* (a phrase of melody which is immediately repeated but at a higher or lower pitch).

The melodic shape of the first four bars of score 1

1 *Praeludium* for violin and piano

Pugnani-Kreisler

When score-reading, you will find that noticing the **rhythm** of the notes (distinguishing especially between long notes and short notes) helps you to keep your place as much as noticing how they rise and fall in pitch. In the score above, the melody flows in even crotchets, and the notes move mainly by leap. In the next score, however, the notes move mainly by step – and several different note-values are used: minims, crotchets (both plain and dotted), and quavers (see chart 1, page 92).

The time signature again shows four crotchet beats to a bar. But as you follow this score, to keep with the music your eye will need to linger

The melodic shape of the first four bars of score 2

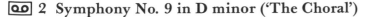

slightly when you see and hear minims (worth two beats), and move more quickly when you see and hear quavers (each worth only half a beat).

The curved line joining two notes of the same pitch at bars 12-13, and again at bars 20-21, is called a **tie**. You will hear a single sustained sound, which lasts for the value of both notes added together.

Beethoven builds up this melody in phrases of four bars each. Often, a bar of music - or even a group of bars - is used more than once during the melody. Spot as many of these repetitions as you can.

2 Symphony No. 9 in D minor ('The Choral') — *Beethoven (1770–1827)*

The melody-line score below presents rather more of a challenge. Prepare your listening first by investigating the score. Notice:

(a) the tempo marking, and time signature (see chart 3, page 92);
(b) the terms, signs and abbreviations printed below the melody;
(c) the general contour of the melody - rising and falling in pitch;
(d) occasions when Brahms uses *sequence* (e.g. the first four bars of the melody are repeated at a lower pitch in bars 5-8);
(e) the rhythms and the various note-values used (in several bars, e.g. bar 2, the first two notes are *tied* - you see five notes in the bar, but in fact you will hear only four);
(f) occasions where **rests** occur (for every kind of note there is a corresponding sign called a *rest* which indicates an equivalent length of *silence* - see chart 1, page 92).

3 Violin Sonata No. 3 in D minor — *Brahms (1833–97)*

5

There are several points to notice in the next score before you follow it as the music is played. First, notice that this extract ends with a **repeat sign** - a double bar-line with a pair of dots in front of it - here meaning 'repeat from the beginning' (see chart 6, page 93).

Mozart heads his music *Menuetto* (Minuet), without giving a precise tempo marking. The speed, though, will be fairly quick - too quick for your eye to take in the four semiquavers (♪♪♪♪) in bar 1 as separate notes. In a fastish tempo, when you see a group of quick notes like this, take them in *as a group*, rather than individually.

In the third bar, the figure *3* beneath the joined quavers indicates a *triplet* - meaning that the three notes are to be performed evenly in the time of two notes of the same kind.

As you listen to this music, you will find that there are several 'landmarks' in the score - points at which you can check that you are keeping your place. For example:
  each time the group of semiquavers (♪♪♪♪) occurs,
  or the jerky rhythm of dotted quaver + semiquaver (♪. ♪);
  each time a trill (*tr*) is marked,
  or the music is marked to be played loudly (*f*) - especially the first
    note of bar 9, at which point the melody leaps to its highest note.

4 *Menuetto* (bars 1–20) from Serenade for 13 Wind Instruments   *Mozart (1756–91)*

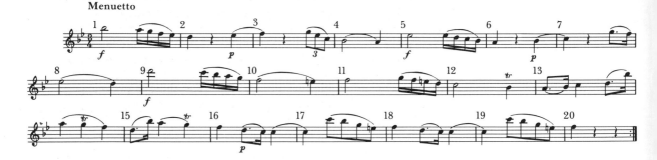

Assignment 1 **A** Investigate the melody-line score printed below, noting as many points as possible to prepare your listening.

B Follow the score as the music is played.

5 Ballet Music in G major from *Rosamunde*   *Schubert (1797–1828)*

Assignment 2

Listen again to the music by Schubert, following the melody-line score.

1 Which family of instruments plays during the first part of this music?
2 Which instruments take over later? At which bar does this happen?
3 Explain these words, signs and abbreviations used in this score:

Andantino $\frac{2}{4}$:|| 𝄞   𝄢   *p*   *mf*   *cresc.*   𝄐

4 Look at the drawings of melodic shapes on pages 4 and 5. Then close this book and, as you listen to Schubert's melody, draw the melodic shape of the first few bars. Afterwards, compare your drawing with the rise and fall in pitch of the notes printed in the score.
5 Draw each kind of note-value used in this score. Make a list, arranging your note-values in the order of longest to shortest. Then name each one, and give its value in relation to the beat.
6 There are certain melodic and rhythmic patterns which are used more than once in this score. Give the bar numbers where these repetitions occur.

Assignment 3

For practice, follow other melody-line scores as you listen to the music.

Checklist 1

Main points to remember

Before listening:

- Always prepare your listening first by looking carefully through the score.
- Look at the tempo (speed) marking – this will give you an idea of how quickly your eye will need to travel to keep up with the music.
- Take note of the time signature, which indicates the number of beats to each bar.
- Look through carefully for repeat signs, or any other indications that sections of music are to be repeated.
- Notice where any Italian words or abbreviations are used in the score; make sure you know the meaning of these, and any other musical signs and symbols, before following the score.

As you follow the score:

- Always use your eyes and ears to help each other – matching what you *see* to what you *hear*.
- Watch for the general rise and fall in the pitch of the notes. Look for: wide leaps; notes which climb or fall by step; notes which are repeated and so remain at the same pitch; sequences.
- Sense the first beat of each bar; unless there is a change of speed or time signature, the bar-lines should 'arrive' regularly – regardless of the number of notes in each bar.
- Notice especially where lengthy notes occur; and tied notes; and notes of very short value. Take in a group of quick notes *as a group* – rather than as individual notes.
- Watch for dotted notes forming jerky rhythmic patterns (e.g. ♩.♪♩.♪).
- Notice where rests occur.
- Certain 'landmarks' in the score will help you to check that you are keeping your place (or to find your place again should you get lost!); for example – wide leaps; trills, and other ornaments; a distinctive rhythmic pattern or a group of notes which is repeated; a sequence; certain dynamic markings (see chart 5, page 93).

3
Music for piano

Systems

Music for piano is printed on two staves. Look at the beginning of the piano piece by Chopin, printed below. The upper stave, with the treble clef, carries the music to be played by the pianist's right hand. The lower stave, with the bass clef, has the music for the left hand. The two staves are joined together on the left by a vertical line, and also by a curved bracket. Staves joined together in this way by a vertical line make what is called a **system**. And so this piano piece is printed in four systems.

Assignment 4

Look carefully through the score before you listen to this music. The small note with a line through its stem, at bars 11 and 19, is an *acciaccatura* (a 'crushed' note). It is played quickly on, or just before, the beat. Discover the meaning of any other musical signs, words or abbreviations which may be new to you by referring to the charts and tables printed at the end of this book (especially charts 5, 7, and 11).

Assignment 5

Following a score of music for piano means following two staves at once. However, this piece by Chopin is not too difficult to follow. At the beginning of the music, after each melody note is sounded, immediately glance down to the chords played by the pianist's left hand. This will help you to keep your place. Use your ears and eyes to help each other – for example: you will hear, and see, when the harmony changes. When you notice several notes to each bar in the right hand, you may find it best to keep your eye on the upper stave only.

Prelude in E minor, Op. 28 No. 4   *Chopin (1810–49)*

Assignment 6

Follow the scores of other piano pieces as you listen to the music.

4
Chamber music scores

Chamber music is music written for a small group of solo musicians, and intended to be played in a room, or chamber, rather than a large hall. Whatever combination of instruments may be involved, there is only one instrument for each part included in the score. The two-stave score below is from a trio by Beethoven. A trio, of course, is for three instruments, and in this work they are a clarinet, cello and piano – but in this particular variation from the final movement, the piano remains silent while the clarinet and cello play a duet.

Assignment 7　Investigate the score below. Notice:
(a) the number of systems taken up by the music;
(b) the clef which each instrument uses;
(c) the time signature, indicating the number of beats to each bar;
(d) the rests in the clarinet part;
(e) the phrasing and dynamic markings which Beethoven adds to his score;
(f) Beethoven's use of *imitation* - each time the clarinet enters, it 'imitates' the phrase which the cello has just played.

Assignment 8 A　Follow the score as you listen to the music. Follow the cello part when there are rests for the clarinet. When you see and hear notes played by the clarinet, follow that stave until the next group of rests occurs.

B　Follow the score again – but this time, when the instruments play together, try to keep an eye on both staves at once.

🔊 Variation II from the third movement of Trio in B flat, Op. 11
Beethoven (1770–1827)

Cello　　*Clarinet*

Violin

The next score, part of a violin sonata by Beethoven, needs three staves: one for the violin, and two for the piano. However, as you follow the score you will find that you really only need to divide your attention between the violin part (the upper stave of each system) and the music played by the pianist's right hand (the stave immediately below the violin part).

In this score, red arrows have been added to indicate the first note of each new 'event' in the music. As the red arrows show, Beethoven shares the musical interest equally between piano and violin. At first there are quite lengthy stretches where each instrument in turn takes the main interest. But later, beginning at bar 33, musical ideas are passed more swiftly between the two instruments – as shown by the red arrows now changing more frequently from stave to stave.

Assignment 9 **A** Before listening to this music, examine the beginning of the score. Beethoven's tempo marking indicates that the speed should be 'at a walking speed, rather fastish'. Notice the time signature – two beats to a bar. Then hear in your mind (or tap out) the rhythm of the opening four bars.

B As the music is played, follow the route traced through the score by the red arrows.

▭▭ Slow movement (bars 1–64) from Violin Sonata No. 2 in A *Beethoven (1770–1827)*

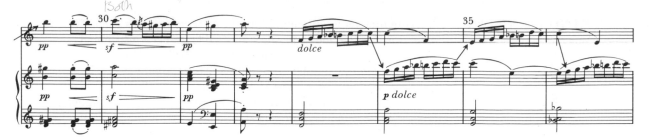

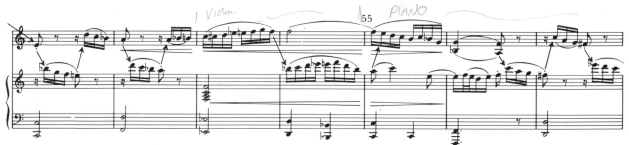

Assignment 10

1 Explain the time signature used in this score.
2 Name the musical device which Beethoven uses from bar 33 onwards.
   (At bar 33, the violin 'leads'; at bar 41, it is the piano's turn.)
3 Explain these musical signs and abbreviations from Beethoven's score:

p pp ─────── ─────── fp sf *dolce* ♪

11

THE STRING QUARTET

A **string quartet** is written for two violins, a viola, and a cello. The score is printed on four separate staves – one for each instrument. Notice that the viola part is written in the alto 'C' clef (or 'viola clef') in which the middle line of the stave is middle C.

The score shown here – the Minuet section from the third movement of Mozart's String Quartet No. 19 in C – presents three special challenges. First, the music moves quite quickly. Secondly, there are repeats to observe. And thirdly, each instrument, at some time during the music, takes the main interest (though you may find at times that the high 1st violin tries to claim attention when, in fact, the main interest really lies in one of the lower parts of the musical texture).

The alto 'C' clef (or 'viola clef'):

middle C →

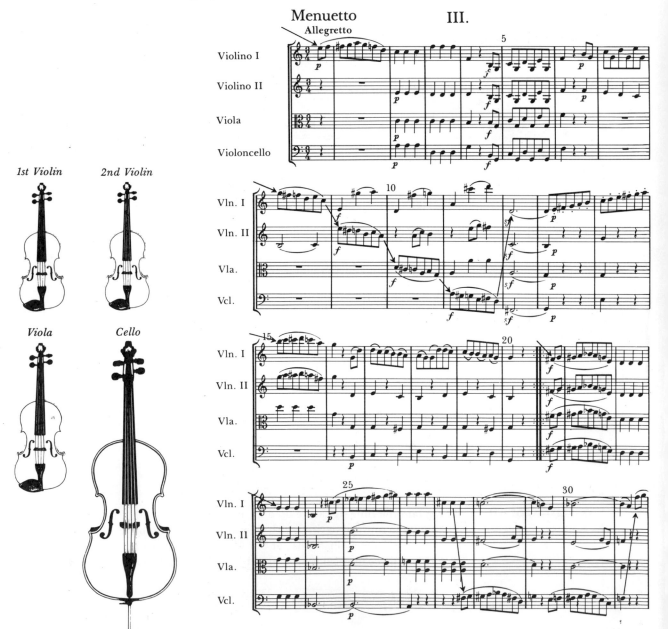

Minuet from String Quartet in C, K465 ('The Dissonance') *Mozart (1756–91)*

1st Violin

2nd Violin

Viola

Cello

Assignment 11 **A** Look carefully through the score of this music by Mozart. Notice:

 (a) the repeat signs – and especially the point in the score to which, as each repeat is taken, your eye needs to *return*;

 (b) the way in which, to follow the musical interest, your eye needs to pass from stave to stave, up and down through the texture of the music – as shown by the red arrows added to the score.

 B As the music is played, follow the route indicated through the score by the red arrows.

QUINTET

The chamber music score on pages 15 and 16 shows the first half of the slow movement from Mozart's Quintet for piano and wind instruments. A quintet is music written for five soloists, and the instruments which take part in this quintet are a piano, three woodwind instruments (oboe, clarinet, and bassoon), and a brass instrument (a horn).

'Transposing' instruments

Two of the wind instruments here – the clarinet and the horn – are examples of what are known as 'transposing' instruments. These are instruments whose notes are *written* at a different pitch than they actually *sound* when they are played. This need present no problem to you as you follow the score, since to keep with the music your eye needs only to recognise the rise and fall of the notes and the rhythms. But the following is an explanation of what is in fact happening.

The clarinet

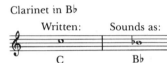

Clarinet in B♭

Written: Sounds as:

C   B♭

When transposing instruments are mentioned in scores, always bear in mind the note C. This score mentions the clarinet as being 'in B♭'. This means that when the note C is *written*, the clarinet actually *sounds* the note B♭. When D is written, the note sounded will be C; and so on. So a clarinet 'in B♭' (and also a trumpet 'in B♭') sounds notes *a tone lower* than those written in the score. (See chart 8, page 94.)

The horn

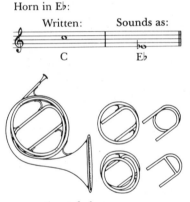

Horn in E♭:

Written: Sounds as:

C   E♭

An early horn, with crooks

Until valves were invented (around 1820) the horn consisted of a single length of tubing, and the notes it could play were rather limited. Horn players needed a set of 'crooks', any one of which could be fixed into the horn temporarily to alter the overall length of tube and so provide a new set of notes. A composer would write the horn parts in the key of C, then say which crook was to be used. The sounds then automatically came out in the correct key. The score opposite mentions 'Horn in E♭', so the player would use the E♭ crook. This means that when the note C is *written*, the horn will *sound* E♭, a major 6th below. (And so the first note of the horn part, written as G, in fact sounds as the B♭ below.)

Written:

Sounding:

Horn in D   Horn in E♭   Horn in F

Assignment 12

Prepare your listening by investigating the score before the music is played. Points to notice in this score include:

(a) The order in which the parts for the five instruments are printed from top to bottom of each system.

(b) The tempo marking, and the time signature. As the music begins, you will sense three steady quaver beats to each bar. In bar 1, for example, the oboe has two quavers, followed by a group of four demisemiquavers to be fitted into the remaining quaver beat.

(c) Ornaments. Besides **trills** (𝄉) there are also **turns** (marked ∾). When these signs occur in the score, you will *hear* more notes than you *see*. For example, here is bar 19 from the score, (a) as it is printed, and (b) as the clarinettist will actually play it:

(a) [Clarinet]   (b)

Assignment 13   As the music is played, follow the route through the score traced by the red arrows, indicating the main points of interest. However, at various times during the music you will hear *other* interesting things going on, some of which have been picked out with red brackets. When these occur, try to keep an eye on more than one stave at once. Use your eyes and ears to help each other – identifying the sound of each instrument and relating what you *see* to what you *hear*.

This is the first score in which you need to turn the page during the course of the music. Be ready for this! It is always best to turn over slightly in advance, rather than leave it too late and be left behind.

Larghetto (bars 1–43) from the Quintet for piano and wind instruments

Mozart (1756–91)

Oboe

Clarinet

Modern valve horn

Bassoon

Special Assignment A

Each of these two scores presents music for four solo instruments. Your assignment here is first to investigate each score, discovering:

(a) the instruments which take part;

(b) the number of staves to each system, and the number of systems to a page;

(c) any indications that sections of music are to be repeated;

(d) the placing, and meaning, of any Italian words or abbreviations. [Refer to the charts and tables at the end of this book to discover the meaning of anything which may be new to you.]

Then follow each score as the music is played. Remember: always use your eyes and ears to help each other, matching what you *see* to what you *hear*.

1 Minuet from String Quartet in A Major*   *Hofstetter (?–1785)*

This piece is recorded on *Form and Design* Cassette 1.

(1) As you listen to this piece for the first time, follow the music played by the 1st violin.

(2) Listen to the music again, now following the 2nd violin part.

(3) Listen once more – this time keeping an eye on *both* these parts by glancing from one stave to the other.

* Until recently, this String Quartet was thought to be by Haydn.

2 Slow movement from Flute Quartet (K285) *Mozart (1756–91)*

This piece is recorded on *Form and Design* Cassette 1.

As you investigate the flute part of this score (the highest stave of each system) notice the single-note ornaments printed in small music type (for example: bar 2, and bars 4–7). Each of these is called an *appoggiatura* (a 'leaning' note) which, as you will hear, is played *on* the beat, and steals its value from the main note which follows it.

(1) Listen to this piece, following the flute part. There are many wide leaps which will help you to check that you are keeping your place.

(2) Listen to the music again, this time following the cello part (the lowest stave of each system). Very often, the cellist plays a *pizzicato* quaver on each beat followed by a quaver rest; but notice where longer rests occur – for example: bars 8 and 13, and bars 16 and 24. (During these rests, glance upwards to see and hear what other instruments are playing.) The semiquaver patterns, which the cellist plays in bars 5–7 and 29–30, are good 'landmarks' in the score at which to check that you are keeping your place.

Flute

18

(3) Listen to the music once more, this time keeping an eye on both the
flute part *and* the cello part (and perhaps, at times, glancing at
the inner parts to take in even more detail).

5
The orchestral score

The music printed opposite is the opening page from the score of a colourful work for orchestra called 'Spanish Caprice' by the Russian composer Rimsky-Korsakov. Instruments are arranged down the page of an orchestral score according to the four sections of the orchestra, in the order: **woodwind**, **brass**, **percussion**, **strings**. If a harp is included, its music comes between the percussion and the strings. If voices are used, or there is an important solo instrument – as, for instance, in a piano or violin concerto – then these staves of music are placed immediately above the strings. (In older scores, though, voice parts may be printed between the violas and cellos, so splitting the string section in two.)

On the first page of a score, the staves are labelled (usually in a foreign language) with the names of the instruments taking part. On other pages, however, abbreviations only may be used – or perhaps no identification offered at all. (Chart 12 on page 97 lists the names of most instruments found in orchestral scores, and their abbreviations, in four languages.)

Systems and brackets

Notice, on the score printed opposite, the continuous vertical line, running down the left-hand side. This links all the staves together to make what is called a system. A thick bracket marks off the staves for the woodwind instruments, another links the brass staves, and a third links those for the strings – so the eye can pick out each family of instruments at a glance. Some editions of scores lack these brackets, but even so there will usually be a break in the bar-lines between the families of instruments. In this score there are extra, smaller, brackets indicating pairs of staves for similar instruments – 1st and 2nd violins, piccolo and flutes, the two horn staves, and so on.

Most scores begin by showing staves for all the instruments which will take part – even those which may have no notes to play on the first page. On succeeding pages, however, it is usual to save space (and also expense) by only printing staves for those instruments which are actually playing at the time. The number of systems therefore varies from one page to another – sometimes a single system to a page, sometimes two or more. In many scores, two slanting parallel lines are printed between systems, warning you as you arrive at a fresh page that it carries more than one system. (See pages 53–6 of this book.) In some editions, though, the only warning you may be given is that there is a break in the vertical line down the left-hand side of the page.

Clefs

Notice, on the page of score printed opposite, the four different kinds of clef which are used. The two used most often are the treble clef and the bass clef; but the viola part is written in the 'alto C clef' (or 'viola clef'), and the tenor trombone part is written in the 'tenor C clef'. Here is the note middle C, written in each of these four clefs:

Treble clef,
or G clef

Bass clef,
or F clef

Alto C clef,
or viola clef

Tenor C clef

CAPRICCIO ESPAGNOL

I. Alborada

N. Rimsky-Korsakov, Op. 34
[1844–1908]

Assignment 14
1. In which order are the sections of the orchestra arranged down the page of a full orchestral score?
2. Mention two ways in which it might be made clear to your eye which staves belong to each family of instruments.

Assignment 15
1. Give the English name for each instrument included in the score shown on page 21.
2. Which instruments in the score have their parts written on a single line rather than on a five-line stave? Why?

Assignment 16
Each box below gives the instruments included in the score of a famous composition. First, list the instruments in English (charts 12 and 10 will help you). Then draw brackets against each of your lists, as shown on the left of page 21, to group the instruments into the four sections of the orchestra.

Danse Macabre by Camille Saint-Saëns	*Till Eulenspiegel* by Richard Strauss	*The Fountains of Rome* by Ottorino Respighi
1 Petite flûte	Kleine Flöte	Flauto piccolo
2 Grandes flûtes	3 Grosse Flöten	2 Flauti
2 Hautbois	3 Hoboen	2 Oboi
2 Clarinettes en *si bémol*	Englisches Horn	Corno inglese
2 Bassons	Klarinette in D	2 Clarinetti in *si bemolle*
4 Cors (2 en *sol*, 2 en *ré*)	2 Klarinetten in B	Clarinetto basso in *la*
2 Trompettes en *ré*	Bassklarinette in B	2 Fagotti
2 Trombones	3 Fagotte	4 Corni in *fa*
Xylophone	Kontrafagott	2 Trombe in *si bemolle*
3 Timbales en *ré, la, sol*	4 Hörner in F	3 Tromboni
Triangle	3 Trompeten in F	Tuba
Cymbales	3 Posaunen	Timpani
Grosse caisse	Tuba	Triangolo
Harpe	Pauken	Piatti
Violon solo	Becken	Campanette
1ers Violons	Triangel	1 Campana
2ds Violons	Grosse Trommel	Celesta
Altos	Kleine Trommel	Pianoforte
Violoncelles	erste Violinen	2 Arpe
Contrebasses	zweite Violinen	Violino I
	Bratschen	Violino II
	Violoncelle	Viola
	Kontrabässe	Violoncello
		Contrabasso

Assignment 17
1. In score-reading, what does the word *system* refer to?
2. Look through various kinds of score, and see how many systems there are to a page. How can you tell when a page carries more than one system?

Strings

The string section of the orchestra is made up of five groups of instruments. There are two groups of violins, called 1st violins and 2nd violins – the 1st violins usually playing higher notes than the 2nds. The other three groups are the violas, cellos, and double basses.

The strings are the 'backbone' of the orchestra (more than half the members of an orchestra play string instruments) and you will find that in many orchestral scores the main interest is given to the 1st violins.

In the music by Mozart, printed below, only four staves are needed for the five groups of instruments. 1st and 2nd violins have a stave each. The third stave down is for the violas. And cellos and double basses share the lowest stave, since in this piece (as in most music composed before 1800) the double basses merely 'double', or duplicate, the notes played by the cellos.

However, double basses are 'transposing' instruments. Their notes are always written one octave higher than they actually sound. So although, in the score below, cellos and basses play from the same *written* notes, the double basses will in fact sound one octave lower than the cellos.

Assignment 18

Follow the score below as the music is played. As each section of music is played for the first time, follow the 1st violin stave. During each repeat, choose one of the other staves to follow instead.

'Romanze' (bars 1–16) from *Eine Kleine Nachtmusik*   *Mozart (1756–91)*

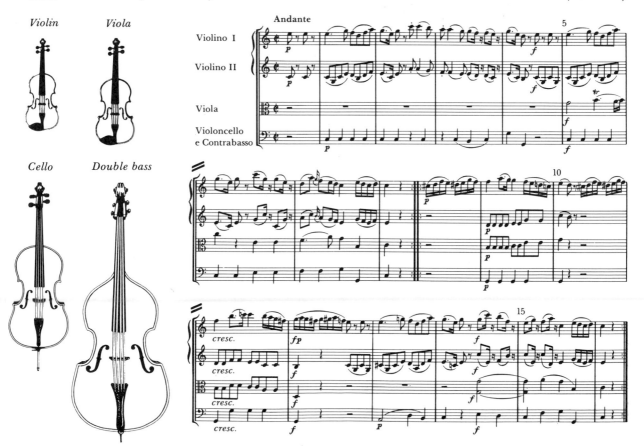

Violin *Viola* *Cello* *Double bass*

23

Music for strings on five staves

The score on these two pages shows the first half of a piece for strings by the Norwegian composer, Grieg. Before listening to the music, examine the score. In this piece, five staves are needed for the strings, since the double basses play different notes from the cellos, and so must be given a stave of their own.

As suits the title of the piece, the music is in a minor key, and the pace is fairly slow (♩=50, following the tempo marking, indicates 50 crotchet beats per minute). Violins, violas and cellos are marked *con sordini*, meaning 'with mutes' – a comb-like device is clipped onto the bridge, damping the vibrations to give a hushed, silvery tone.

Grieg builds up this first half of his music with repetitions of an eight-bar phrase – each time higher in pitch, and rising to a climax. The third playing of the phrase (beginning at bar 17) is extremely rich and sonorous. 1st violins, 2nd violins and violas each divide into two groups, one group playing the upper notes on the stave and the other group playing the lower notes. At the same time, the cellos divide into three groups (*divisi a 3*).

Assignment 19   Listen to this music, following the 1st violin part throughout.

🔲 'The Death of Åse' (bars 1–24) from *Peer Gynt* Suite 1   *Grieg (1843–1907)*

Violin

Assignment 20

Cello

You probably found the 1st violin part fairly easy to follow since these instruments are carrying the melody and sound at the top of the musical texture. But in this piece the cellos, too, have a very melodious part to play.

Listen to the music again – this time following the cello part. This is a good piece for concentrating your listening lower down in the texture of the music. Keep your eyes on the cello part (the second stave up on each system of this score) and direct your ears to pick out sounds from the musical texture to match the notes you *see*. When you arrive at bar 17, where the cellos divide into three groups, follow (and listen for) the notes played by the highest group of cellos.

Strings + wind

The score opposite shows the beginning of the slow first movement of a Haydn symphony. The music is scored for two cors anglais (woodwind), two horns (brass), and strings. Both types of wind instrument used here are 'transposing' instruments (see page 14). The horns are *'in Es'* (E♭), meaning that when the note C is written, the note sounded is E♭ below.

The pitch of a cor anglais lies five notes lower than that of an oboe. The method of fingering is exactly the same on both instruments, and so all oboists are equally able to play the cor anglais. Therefore, to make things straightforward for the player, in cor anglais music all the notes are written five notes higher than they actually sound. This means the player reads, and fingers, the notes exactly as if they were written for oboe, but they automatically sound a fifth lower at the correct pitch for cor anglais.

Assignment 21

Examine the score, noticing especially:
(a) the pairs of slanting parallel lines (⫽) making clear how many systems of music there are on the page.
(b) the repeat marks at the end of the extract;
(c) the two kinds of grace-note played by the violins at bars 14-19: *acciaccatura* (see page 8), and *appoggiatura* (see page 18);
(d) the notes at bars 10 and 11, in the 2nd violin and viola parts, which are printed with slashes through their stems – a kind of 'musical shorthand' indicating that each note is to be repeated a certain number of times (see chart 9, page 95);
(e) places in the score where *a 2.* is marked (e.g. bar 3, cor anglais part). This indicates that the two instruments sharing the stave are to play the same notes in unison (whereas, in bars 1 and 2, each of the horns is given separate notes to play).

Assignment 22

Follow the score as the music is played. Your eyes will be guided by the red arrows, but let your ears also be aware of the bass, treading along in steady quavers. From bar 14 onwards it would be possible to follow just the 1st violin part, but spare a glance for the phrases played by the cors anglais, picked out with red brackets – returning your eye, between these phrases, to the 1st violin stave by finding the trill and matching what you see to what you hear.

Assignment 23

1 This music is in E♭ major, which has a key signature of three flats. Which instruments in the score are given a *different* key signature. Why?
2 Which instruments are played *con sordini*? What does this mean?
3 Which section of the orchestra is not represented in this score?
4 At the beginning of this music, all the strings play 'in unison' – they play the same notes, even though they may sound one or more octaves apart. At which bar does this cease to happen?
5 (a) How many notes do the 2nd violins play in bar 11? What is the value of each note?
  (b) How many notes do the violas play on the third beat of bar 10? What is the value of each note?
6 Name *three* transposing instruments included in this score. For each type of instrument, write out the first two notes printed in the score:
  (a) at the pitch they are written; (b) at the pitch they actually sound.

Cor anglais

Horn

The next score is of music for strings with important solo parts for an oboe and a horn. The horn is 'in D', meaning that when C is written the note sounded will be the note D, seven notes lower. The music on the lowest stave, labelled simply as *Basso* ('bass'), is intended to be played by cellos, double basses (sounding one octave lower), and possibly bassoon as well.

This extract begins with a solo for the oboe. At bar 55, the strings play a short linking passage leading to a solo for the horn, beginning at bar 57. From bar 61, the musical interest is divided between the oboe ('shadowed' by the horn) and the 1st violins.

At bars 68–70, Mozart builds up excitement by giving the strings quickly repeated notes (printed in abbreviated form – see chart 9, page 95). Notice, at bar 71, the sign ⌢ which appears above each stave. In each of the string parts the sign is used to mean 'pause', indicating that the rest above which it appears should be held on for longer than its normal value. In the oboe and horn parts, however, the same sign is used to indicate that the soloists are to play a short, unaccompanied **Cadenza** **cadenza** – a fairly showy passage, often based on one or more tunes heard earlier, displaying the players' technical ability. Usually a player was expected to improvise a cadenza on the spot – though in this music, as two players are involved, it would very likely be worked out between them in advance. A cadenza invariably ended with a fairly lengthy trill (printed here as the third beat of bar 71) on a note of the dominant chord – the chord based on the fifth note of the scale. This served as a signal to the orchestra to begin playing again.

Assignment 24

Follow the score as the music is played. During the opening bars the solo oboe takes the main musical interest, but glance down to the lowest stave to notice the *imitation* in the bass-part – you will certainly hear it. When the cadenza is played, listen out for the trill and be ready for the strings to re-enter. From that point to the end of the score, the violin parts interweave, alternately rising and falling. If, when you are score-reading, you find a passage like this rather involved to follow, look for a simpler line to follow instead – for example, the bass part.

Assignment 25

Listen to the music again, and answer these questions:

1 Which instrument plays the first phrase of the cadenza? Which plays the second phrase?

2 These phrases are based on a phrase from earlier in this score. In which bars does it first appear?

3 Imagine you are one of the string players. How would you recognise that the soloists are coming to the end of their cadenza?

Oboe

Horn

The Concerto

A concerto is a work in which the sound of a solo instrument - or sometimes, a small group of instruments - is contrasted against the more powerful sound of an orchestra. (The word may come from Italian, meaning 'get together'; or from Latin, meaning 'dispute'.) A solo concerto is usually in three movements: fairly fast; slow; fast. The score printed on the next four pages shows the beginning of the slow second movement of a concerto by Mozart.

Mozart scores this concerto for solo piano, strings, and wind (five woodwind and two brass instruments). The horns are 'in C', and so you might expect their notes to sound at the pitch at which they are written. But things are not *quite* so straightforward! These horns in fact behave in exactly the same way as the double basses: a written C will sound as C - but one octave lower.

Assignment 26

Look through the four pages of score, taking note of:
(a) the names of the instruments taking part;
(b) the order in which their staves are arranged from top to bottom of the first system of the score (especially noticing the placing of the solo part - immediately above the 1st violin part);
(c) the thick brackets down the left-hand side, grouping the staves according to the three sections of orchestra represented;
(d) the number of systems on each page of score;
(e) the figure 1 printed in bar 6, and again in bar 9, indicating that the notes are to be played by the principal player only of each pair.

Assignment 27

1 Make a list, in English, of the instruments which take part in this music. (The score begins by showing staves for all the instruments - even those which, at first, are given no notes to play.)
2 In each system after the first, staves are printed for only those instruments which are playing at the time.
   (a) Which instrument is not represented in systems 2 to 6 of the score?
   (b) Which instruments are not represented in each system on page 34?
3 (a) Which clef is used for the bassoon notes in bar 9?
   (b) What would be printed at bar 9 if Mozart wanted both bassoons to play these notes in unison?

Assignment 28

Listen to the music, following the score. The red arrows point out the main events in the music, though at times you may hear other interesting things going on elsewhere. When you notice these occurring, identify the sounds of the instruments concerned and find their music within the system. Remember the 'score order' - woodwind staves will be found in the upper part of a system; string staves in the lower part, with those for the violins marked with an extra (curved) bracket.

Mozart often played the solo part in performances of his piano concertos, while at the same time conducting the orchestra from the keyboard. In the recording heard on the cassette, the soloist and the conductor is Vladimir Ashkenazy.

Slow movement (bars 1–44) from Piano Concerto in G (K453)   *Mozart (1756–91)*

II.

Minuet and Trio

When a Classical composer such as Haydn or Mozart wrote a work in four movements (for example, a symphony, or a string quartet) he planned the third movement as a Minuet and Trio. Beethoven later transformed this into the much brisker and more vigorous Scherzo and Trio (*scherzo* meaning 'joke') but still kept to the same basic plan.

One of the special challenges when following the score of a piece like this is to observe **repeat markings** (see chart 6, page 93).

The overall design of a piece in Minuet and Trio form is *ternary*, meaning that it is built up in three main sections of music, A B A:

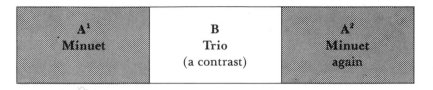

But both the Minuet and the Trio are each in two parts, with each part marked to be repeated (see the score on the next two pages). Composers did not bother to write out the Minuet again after the Trio. Instead, they simply wrote *Menuetto D.C.* – 'Minuet again from the beginning'. However, the custom was to *omit* any repeats in the Minuet when it was played again after the Trio.

So a performance of a Minuet and Trio goes like this:

Minuet:	part one – with repeat part two – with repeat	} **A¹**
Trio:	part one – with repeat part two – with repeat	} **B**
Minuet:	part one – *without* repeat part two – *without* repeat	} **A²**

It is always wise to investigate very thoroughly the score of a Minuet and Trio (or a Scherzo and Trio) before the music is played, and take careful note of where repeats will occur. The Minuet and Trio by Haydn, overleaf, conveniently fits onto two facing pages of score. But a longer piece may take up several pages of score, involving several page-turns – not only moving forwards through the score, but also turning *back* as well.

Assignment 29   **A**   Investigate the score of the Minuet and Trio by Haydn, printed on the next two pages. Look to see which instruments take part (you will also hear a harpsichord, filling out the harmonies, and a bassoon doubling the cello part). Notice especially where repeat markings occur (in this score these have been picked out in red to help you).

  B   Follow the score as the music is played. Be ready for the repeats! But remember – repeats are *omitted* when the Minuet is played again after the Trio.

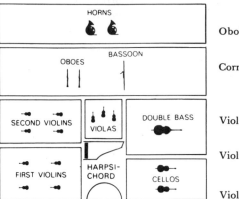 Minuet and Trio from Symphony No. 21 in A *Haydn (1732–1809)*

Assignment 30

1 Hearing the first four bars of this Minuet by Haydn probably reminded you of the beginning of another famous Minuet by Mozart (composed 23 years later). In which of Mozart's compositions does it occur?

2 How many times during the performance of this Minuet and Trio by Haydn does the orchestra play:
   (a) the first eight bars of the Trio?
   (b) the first eight bars of the Minuet?

3 What does *a 2.* mean, printed above the music for the oboes at bar 1? Why is this instruction not printed above the music for horns at bar 5?

4 What is the meaning of *Oboi e Corni tacent*, printed at the beginning of the Trio?

5 In a movement of this kind, there is usually some kind of musical contrast between the Minuet and the Trio. Mention three ways in which the Trio presents a contrast to the Minuet in this movement by Haydn.

Special Assignment B

The score in this Special Assignment shows the music of the Minuet and Trio from Beethoven's Septet in E♭. First, refresh your memory about the way a piece like this is performed by looking again at page 35.

Then prepare your listening by investigating the score. Notice:
(a) the instruments which are to take part, and the clef used by each one;
(b) the order in which the instruments are arranged from top to bottom of each system in the score;
(c) the number of systems to each page of score;
(d) all markings which indicate that sections of music are to be repeated – noticing in particular those points in the score to which, as each repeat is taken, your eye must very quickly *return*.

Follow the score as the music is played. You will find that although, for much of the time, the violin takes the main musical interest, there are occasions when other instruments are featured instead. When your ear detects this, identify the particular sound and immediately take your eye to that instrument's stave – always matching what you see with what you hear.

After you have listened to this Minuet and Trio following the score, answer these questions:

1 Which 'transposing' instruments take part in this music?
2 Which two instruments are featured in the Trio section of Beethoven's score? To which section of the orchestra does each of these instruments belong?
3 Explain these musical terms and signs found in Beethoven's score:
   Menuetto D.C.   *Fine*   *cresc.*   *p*   *f*   *sf*   *3*   ♪   ￼
4 Four different kinds of clef are used during this score. At which bar does an instrument play a melody written in the tenor 'C' clef? Which instrument is it? Give the letter-names of the first two notes that are played.

Third movement from Septet in E flat, Op. 20

Beethoven (1770-1827)

This piece is recorded on *'Form and Design'* Cassette 2

III.

6
Full orchestra

The diagram shown beside the score on page 36 shows the type and size of orchestra used by Haydn and Mozart in many of their earlier symphonies: a basis of strings, to which were added two horns and a pair of oboes or one or two flutes. It was usually expected that a bassoon would join in, doubling the cello line, and also a harpsichord. This was called the *basso continuo* – the player 'continuing' throughout the music to build chords upon the bass-line (*basso*) to fill out the harmonies and decorate the texture. Sometimes the composer provided a separate bassoon part, and some scores also included two trumpets and a pair of kettle drums.

Towards the end of the 18th century, the four main types of woodwind instrument (flute, oboe, the recently invented clarinet, and bassoon) were combined in pairs to form a self-contained woodwind section. The harpsichord continuo fell out of use, and instead the horns were used to bind together the texture of the music. Very often, trumpets and kettle drums were also included. For some time, this formation of the orchestra was accepted as standard. It is often called the 'Classical orchestra'; it is precisely this combination of instruments which is required in the scores of Haydn's last symphonies and the early orchestral works of Beethoven and Schubert:

THE 'CLASSICAL ORCHESTRA'
(c. 1800)

Woodwind	{	1 or 2 flutes 2 oboes 2 clarinets 2 bassoons
Brass	{	2 horns 2 trumpets
Percussion	{	2 kettle drums
Strings	{	1st violins 2nd violins violas cellos double basses

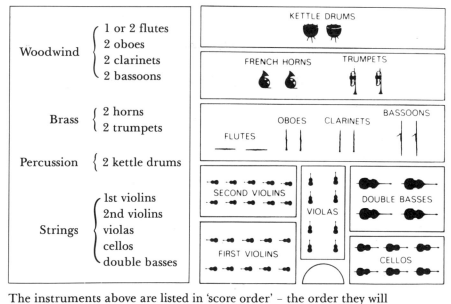

The instruments above are listed in 'score order' – the order they will be arranged from top to bottom of a full page of score. Notice the order of the woodwind instruments. And that the horns appear above the trumpets, even though the trumpets usually play higher notes. This is because the horns are often teamed with the woodwind – blending well, and also binding the sounds together, and so it is an advantage to the eye to have their parts in the score placed immediately below the woodwind staves.

Horns

Early 19th-century composers began to include four horns in their scores, often with one pair 'crooked' in one key and the other pair in another key. This gave a wider range of notes – all of them chosen, of course, so that when transposed they would sound in the key of the piece. After valves were invented (around 1820) it became more usual to write all horn parts for 'horn in F', the notes all sounding a 5th lower than the written pitch. Even today, though, horn parts are still written without key signature. Instead, the accidentals (sharps, flats, and naturals) are written in as they occur in the music.

Trumpets

The trumpet is also a transposing instrument. In older scores, parts are found for trumpets in a variety of keys. Trumpets in B♭ or A transpose downwards – the notes sound lower than they are written. But trumpets in F, D, E, or E♭ transpose *upwards*. (Four examples are included on chart 8, page 94.) The exception is the trumpet in C, whose notes actually sound at the same pitch as they are written. Eventually, it became usual to write for trumpets in B♭, whose notes (like clarinets in B♭) sound one tone lower than they are written.

THE MID 19TH-CENTURY ORCHESTRA

Trombones and tuba

By the mid 19th century, the orchestra had expanded considerably – both in the numbers of instruments employed, and in the range of sounds they could provide. In the brass section, four horns were regularly included and two or three trumpets. Trombones, earlier used only in operas and church music, now found a regular place; and the section was completed by the invention of the tuba. The usual number of trombones in a score is three – most often, two tenor trombones and one bass trombone. (Some scores include alto trombone but this is now obsolete, its part taken by tenor trombone instead.) The two tenor trombones share a stave below the trumpets, and the bass trombone shares the stave beneath with the tuba. (See the score on page 21; you can tell by the key signatures shown that trombones and tuba are not transposing instruments.)

Extra woodwind and percussion

Composers now often included parts for extra woodwind – piccolo, cor anglais, bass clarinet, double bassoon. In some scores, the percussion section still consisted of kettle drums only; but in others, the choice of percussion instruments could be very varied and colourful. Below, you can see the size and range of orchestra needed to play certain scores by mid 19th-century composers. The instruments are listed in score order.

Woodwind	piccolo, 2 flutes, 2 oboes, cor anglais, 2 clarinets, bass clarinet, 2 bassoons, double bassoon
Brass	4 horns, 2, or 3, trumpets, 3 trombones, tuba
Percussion	kettle drums, and other percussion, harp(s)
Strings	1st violins, 2nd violins, violas, cellos, double basses

OTHER PERCUSSION   KETTLE DRUMS (TIMPANI)

HORNS   TRUMPETS   TROMBONES   TUBA

HARPS   BASS CLARINET   CLARINETS   BASSOONS   DOUBLE BASSOON   OBOES   COR ANGLAIS   PICCOLO   FLUTES   DOUBLE BASSES

SECOND VIOLINS   VIOLAS

FIRST VIOLINS   CONDUCTOR   CELLOS

Checklist 2

Hints on following a score for full orchestra
(The points mentioned in Checklist 1, page 7, apply here too.)

Before listening
- Look carefully for any repeat markings.
- Discover which instruments are taking part. (They will be named, usually in a foreign language, on the first page of the score; on other pages, abbreviated names only may be used.)
- Note the tempo (speed) marking, and the time signature.

As you follow the score
- Always be ready for page-turns – it is better to turn over slightly in advance, rather than leave it too late and be left behind.
- Notice at a glance the number of systems (one, or more) to a page. Two or more systems may be separated by slanting lines (⫽) or merely by a break in the vertical line down the left side of the score.
- Within each system, those instruments which are playing will be arranged in 'score order' – woodwind, brass, percussion, strings – with thick brackets and/or a break in the barlines grouping the staves according to these orchestral sections.
- As you listen, identify the sounds of instruments playing the most interesting part at the time, and look for their position within the system according to score order. (In many scores, for much of the time, you will find the main interest lies in the 1st violin part.)
- Be prepared for repeats. Note the point to which your eye needs to *return* (perhaps keeping a finger in the page to negotiate a swift turn-back).

If you should lose your place . . .
- Quickly make sure you haven't miscounted the number of systems to a page, or missed a repeat and should have gone back. If not, it is most likely that you have fallen behind – so skip forward and find a 'landmark' in the score that you are sure you will recognise. *Listen all the time,* and as soon as your ears tell you the music is arriving at that point – quickly latch on, and continue to follow the score.

Assignment 31

The score on the next six pages, from Beethoven's *Egmont Overture*, is written for the 'Classical full orchestra' shown on page 43, but with an extra two horns, and (in the final bars of the overture) the addition of a piccolo. Look through the six pages of this extract.
(a) Note how many systems there are to a page. And how the brackets at the left of each system group staves according to the sections of the orchestra. (Percussion parts are usually printed without a bracket – the eye spots these 'by elimination'.)
(b) Notice that the horns are 'in F and E♭' and the trumpets are 'in F', but that their music is written in the key of C major. And that the composer, having instructed the kettle drum player the note to which each drum should be tuned, then writes out this part without key signature.
(c) Check the score for any unfamiliar signs, words or abbreviations – referring to the charts on pages 92-7 if necessary.
(d) Note the tempo marking and the time signature for this music. Hear in your mind (or tap out) the rhythm of the opening bars – played by 1st violins (bars 1-2), clarinet (bar 3), flute (bar 4).

Assignment 32

Follow the score as the music is played. (Be ready for the page-turns!)

Assignment 33 A The score which begins below is an extract from one of Tchaikovsky's most famous compositions. Here are the instruments needed to perform this piece (though not all of them play in this particular extract):

Piccolo	3 Kettle drums
2 Flutes	Cymbals
2 Oboes	Bass drum
Cor anglais	Harp
2 Clarinets in A	
2 Bassoons	
	1st Violins
4 Horns in F	2nd Violins
2 Trumpets in B♭	Violas
3 Trombones (2 tenor, 1 bass)	Cellos
Tuba	Double basses

Notice that for this music, clarinets 'in A' are used. This means that if the note C is written, the note sounded will be the note A, a minor 3rd (or three semitones) below.

B Refresh your memory by reading the checklists on pages 7 and 45. Then follow the score as the music is performed. In this score there are no red arrows to guide you. Rely instead on your ears and eyes – all the time, concentrating upon picking out and identifying those instruments which sound the most interesting, and immediately locating their position within the system according to score order. You will find in this music in particular that (1) the rise and fall in **pitch** of the notes, and (2) the **rhythm** of the notes (the various note-values in relation to each other – not forgetting 'tied' notes) will help you to follow this score successfully.

Fantasy-Overture: *Romeo and Juliet* **(bars 184–244)**   *Tchaikovsky (1840–93)*

Assignment 34 1 Give the English name for each of these Italian abbreviations:
Vl.   Fl.   Cl.   C.i.   Cb.   Fg.   Cor.   Vc.   A.   Tbn. B.

2 Which instruments in the box on page 52 do not play during this extract?

Assignment 35 1 At the beginning of this extract from Tchaikovsky's score:
(a) What does *con sord.* mean, printed above the viola stave?
(b) In this melody (the famous love-theme) which instrument do the violas 'double'?
(c) Describe how the cellos and double basses are being played.
(d) Which instrument doubles their notes at this point?

2 Beginning on the last beat of bar 192:
(a) Which instruments play the melody?
(b) Give the meaning of *div.* printed above its stave.

3 (a) Name the instruments which play the love-theme at bar 213.
(b) Which instrument plays a counter-melody below?

4 (a) At which bar is the beginning of the love-theme heard again?
(b) Which instruments play the melody?
(c) Name the instruments providing the bass-line of the musical texture.

Assignment 36 Follow this score again, concentrating with eyes and ears to discover even more detail in the music.

7
The vocal score

A **vocal score** is one which shows all the vocal parts of an opera, oratorio, or other work for voices and orchestra – but with all the orchestral parts reduced to a two-stave arrangement which can be played on a piano or organ. Singers use vocal scores when they are learning their parts, and also to rehearse from.

The vocal score on pages 59–62 shows part of the last act of Verdi's opera, *Il Trovatore*. Here is a translation of the Italian words:

Choir [within]: Have mercy upon a soul already near to departing
Upon that journey which knows no return;
Have mercy upon him, Divine Goodness;
Preserve him from becoming a victim of Hell.
Leonora: What terrible sounds I hear! They're prayers for the dying.
They fill the air with darkest terror!
A dreadful foreboding now overpowers me;
It stifles my breathing, and makes my heart beat wildly!
Manrico: Ah! how death is always slow in coming
[from the tower] To one who longs to die!
Farewell, Leonora, farewell!
Leonora: O heaven! I cannot bear it!
Choir [within]: Have mercy upon a soul already near to departing
Upon that journey which knows no return. . .

Assignment 37   Find out about the story of Verdi's opera, *Il Trovatore*, so that you will understand how this extract fits into the plot.

Assignment 38 A   Look through this extract of vocal score. On page 59, the music of the 'choir within' consists of six voice-parts printed on three staves: 1st and 2nd tenors (each marked *divisi* – 'divided into two groups'), and baritones and basses. The mournful tolling of the 'bell for the dying' is sounded as repeated E flats in the accompaniment.

On page 60, bar 10, a rhythmic accompaniment begins and we hear the voice of the heroine of the opera, Leonora. On page 61, at bar 19, the voice of the hero, Manrico, is heard from the distant tower where he is imprisoned. On page 62, notice that the second system of the score needs seven staves – to accommodate the two-stave accompaniment, the voices of Leonora and Manrico, and the six groups of male voices who now continue to chant their prayer for the dying.

B   Follow the score as you listen to the music. Although you will be following a vocal score, you will hear the two-stave accompaniment played by an orchestra. (Notice that the tenor voice-parts are written in the *treble* clef – one octave higher than the actual sounds.)

Assignment 39   After following this music with the score, answer these questions:
1 Which type of voice sings the part of (a) Leonora, and (b) Manrico?
2 Explain the meaning of each of these markings, found in the score:

Andante assai sostenuto   ♩ = 54   *a mezza voce* (bar 1)

𝄐 (bars 15–16)   *3* (bars 17–19)   *Arpa* (bar 19)

'Miserere' (bars 1–30) from Act IV of *I! Trovatore*　　　*Verdi (1813–1901)*

LEONORA

Quel suon, quelle

CORO

sia dell' in - fernal sog - gior - no.

sia dell' in - fernal sog - gior - no.

sia dell' in - fernal sog - gior - no.

L. pre - ci, so - len - ni, fu - ne - ste, empi - ron que-

L. -st'a - e - re di cu - po ter - ror! Conten - de l'am

L -ba - scia, che tut - ta m'in - ve - ste, al lab - bro il re - spi - ro, i pal - pi - ti al

L cor, il re - spi - ro, i pal - pi - ti a il

L cor!

MANRICO (dalla torre)

Ah!.......... Che la mor - te o - gno - ra è.......... tar - da nel ve -

Arpa

8
Full orchestra
+ voices

The score shown on the next eight pages is an extract from the fourth movement of Beethoven's 'Choral' Symphony. For this movement, Beethoven adds voices to the full orchestra – a quartet of solo voices (soprano, alto, tenor, and baritone), and a mixed chorus (sopranos, altos, tenors, and basses). This was the first time that voices were included in a symphony. The words sung are verses Beethoven selected from the poem *An die Freude* ('Ode to Joy') by the German poet, Schiller.

Assignment 40 A Look carefully through the score of this extract. Notice, especially, the score order – the voice-parts are inserted between the violas and the cellos and double basses, with staves for solo voices placed above those for the chorus.

B Find answers to these questions:
1 Which instruments, named on the first page of the score, do not play during this extract?
2 After bar 5, at which bar does the chorus enter? Which group of voices in the chorus sings the melody at this point?
3 At which bar are the four solo voices first heard singing together?
4 Give the meaning of each of these words and abbreviations used by Beethoven in this score:

  p *pizz.* *cresc.* *dim.* *dolce* *sempre f* *arco*

5 Which German musical term does Beethoven use instead of the Italian term *a 2*? At which bars in the score does it appear? To which instruments does it apply?

Assignment 41 Follow the score of this extract as the music is performed. Be ready for the page-turns – but be aware of pages which have two systems of music on them.

Assignment 42 1 If, in this score, neither names nor abbreviations were printed to identify each stave:
  (a) How could you tell that, on page 65, the second stave down belongs to the clarinets?
  (b) How could you tell that, on page 69, the second stave down belongs to the bassoons?
2 Why, in this score, do you see no key signature on the staves for:
  (a) the horns and the trumpets?
  (b) the kettle drums?
3 During this extract, the trumpets play notes of two letter-names only. Name these two notes as they are printed in the score. Which two notes are actually sounded? Is the pitch higher, or lower, than the printed pitch?

Tochter aus E - ly - si - um, wir be - tre - ten feu - er - trunken, Himmli - sche, dein Hei - lig - tum!

Dei - ne Zau - ber bin - den wie-der, was die Mo-de streng geteilt; al - le Menschen wer-den Brü - der,

le Menschen werden Brü - der, wo dein sanfter Flü - gel weilt.

le Menschen werden Brü - der, wo dein sanfter Flü - gel weilt.

le Menschen werden Brü - der, wo dein sanfter Flü - gel weilt.

9
Large orchestra

During the second half of the 19th century, the orchestra increased
still further in size and range. Composers now often wrote for woodwind
instruments in threes or even fours; in some works, extra brass
instruments were included; and, to maintain a balance of sound, there
were more string players to each part.

The music on pages 73-8 is an orchestral extract from Wagner's
The Ring of the Nibelung - a cycle of four operas which he intended to
be performed on four successive evenings. Here are the instruments of
the large orchestra needed to play this piece, given by Wagner on
the opening page of his score:

Kleine Flöte	2 Paar Pauken
3 grosse Flöten	Triangel
3 Hoboen	Becken
Englisches Horn	Rührtrommel
3 Klarinetten in B	
Bassklarinette in B	3 I. Harfen
3 Fagotte	3 II. Harfen
4 Hörner in F, C	
3 Trompeten in F, C	Violinen I
Basstrompete in C	Violinen II
4 Posaunen	Bratschen
2 Tenortuben	Violoncelle
2 Basstuben	Kontrabässe
Kontrabasstuba	

Assignment 43

1 Make a list, in English, of the instruments mentioned in the box above.
2 Look through the extract of the score printed on pages 73-8 and
discover which instruments play on each page. (Notice that on some
pages, when many instruments are playing, wind instruments of the same
type are given one stave only which they must share between them.)

Assignment 44

As the music is played, follow the main route through the score traced
by the red arrows. Even though a very large orchestra is involved
(totalling more than a hundred players), you will probably find that
this score is not at all difficult to follow.

Assignment 45

Give the meaning of each of these abbreviations which Wagner uses to
indicate how his music should be performed:

pp   poco cresc.   più p   1.   zu 2   3   molto cresc.   ff   dim.

Assignment 46

Follow the score again. This time, though, disregard the red arrows and
instead, use your eyes and ears to pick out other interesting details
to be noticed in the music.

FINE

Double Bassoon →

Menuetto D.C.

IV.

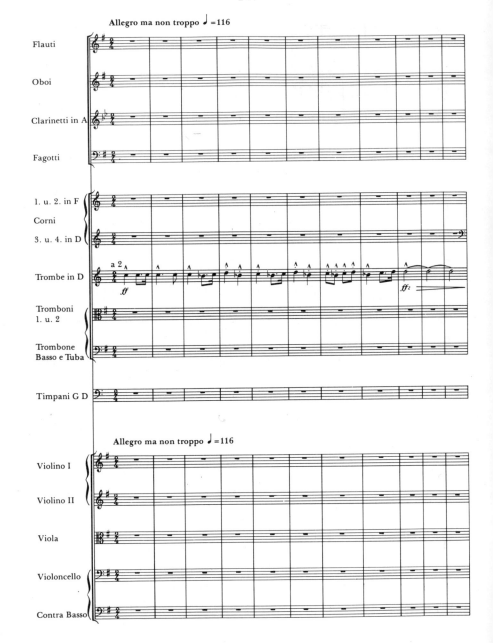

Charts and tables

1 NOTES AND RESTS

Name	Note	Rest	Value when each beat is a crotchet
semibreve (or whole note)	𝅝	——	4 beats
minim (half-note)	𝅗𝅥 or 𝅗𝅥	——	2 beats
crotchet (quarter-note)	𝅘𝅥 or 𝅘𝅥	𝄽 or 𝄽	1 beat
quaver (eighth-note)	𝅘𝅥𝅮 or 𝅘𝅥𝅮	𝄾	½ (2 to a beat)
semiquaver (sixteenth-note)	𝅘𝅥𝅯 or 𝅘𝅥𝅯	𝄿	¼ (4 to a beat)
demisemiquaver (thirty-second-note)	𝅘𝅥𝅰 or 𝅘𝅥𝅰	𝅀	⅛ (8 to a beat)
hemidemisemiquaver (sixty-fourth-note)	𝅘𝅥𝅱 or 𝅘𝅥𝅱	𝅁	$\frac{1}{16}$ (16 to a beat)

A dot placed after a note or rest increases its value by half. If there is a second dot, it will add on half the value of the first.

2 CLEFS

The chart below shows the four different kinds of clef used in scores. In each example, the note shown is middle C.

Treble clef, or 'G' clef

used by instruments of high pitch (e.g. flute, trumpet, and violin)

Bass clef, or 'F' clef

used by instruments of low pitch (e.g. bassoon, tuba, cello, and double bass)

Alto 'C' clef or 'viola clef'

used mainly in music written for viola

Tenor 'C' clef

used for the upper notes of cellos, bassoons, and tenor trombones

3 TIME SIGNATURES

Simple time				Compound time		
Note-value of each beat			Number of beats to each bar	Note-value of each beat		
𝅗𝅥	𝅘𝅥	𝅘𝅥𝅮		𝅗𝅥.	𝅘𝅥.	𝅘𝅥𝅮.
$\frac{2}{2}$ or ¢	$\frac{2}{4}$	$\frac{2}{8}$	2	$\frac{6}{4}$	$\frac{6}{8}$	$\frac{6}{16}$
$\frac{3}{2}$	$\frac{3}{4}$	$\frac{3}{8}$	3	$\frac{9}{4}$	$\frac{9}{8}$	$\frac{9}{16}$
$\frac{4}{2}$	$\frac{4}{4}$ or C	$\frac{4}{8}$	4	$\frac{12}{4}$	$\frac{12}{8}$	$\frac{12}{16}$

4 ACCIDENTALS, AND KEY SIGNATURES

The chart on the right shows the key signatures most often used. In each case, the white note is the tonic (or *doh*) of the major key. The black note is the tonic of its *relative minor* – the minor key sharing the same signature. The leading-note of each minor key is shown in brackets.

♯ sharp	raises the pitch of a note by one semitone
♭ flat	lowers the pitch of a note by one semitone
♮ natural	cancels a previous sharp or flat, restoring the note to its original pitch

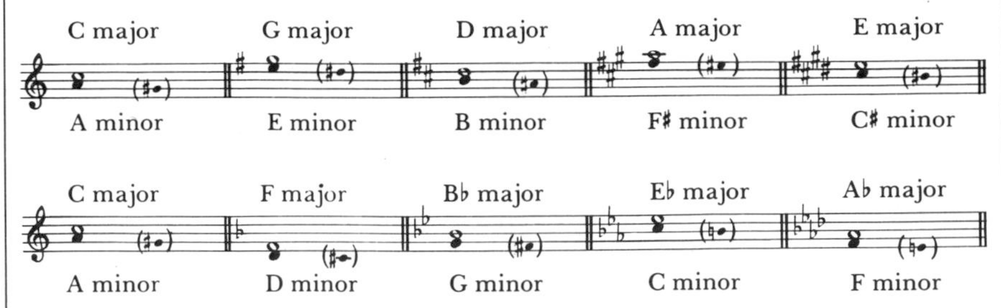

Key signatures chart: C major / A minor, G major / E minor, D major / B minor, A major / F♯ minor, E major / C♯ minor; C major / A minor, F major / D minor, B♭ major / G minor, E♭ major / C minor, A♭ major / F minor.

5 DYNAMIC MARKINGS

Abbreviation	Italian term	English meaning
p	*piano*	soft, quiet
pp	*pianissimo*	very soft
mp	*mezzo piano*	moderately soft
mf	*mezzo forte*	moderately loud
f	*forte*	loud
ff	*fortissimo*	very loud
cresc.	*crescendo*	getting louder
dim. or *dimin.*	*diminuendo*	getting softer
decresc.	*decrescendo*	
fp	*forte-piano*	loud, suddenly followed by soft
fz or *ffz*	*forzato*	forcing the tone, accenting the note
sf or *sfz*	*sforzando*	
sfp	*sforzando-piano*	*sforzando*, suddenly followed by *piano*

A composer may increase the number of 'p's or 'f's; for example, *fff*, 'extremely loud'; or *pppp*, 'as soft as possible'.

6 REPEAT MARKINGS

‖: ‖ Repeat signs. The sign :‖ means repeat from the previous pair of dots – or, if there is none, from the beginning of the piece.

[1.] [2.] '1st time' and '2nd time' at the end of a repeated section. First time, the music beneath [1.] is played. In the repeat, the music beneath [2.] is played instead.

D.C. (*Da Capo*) Repeat 'from the beginning'

D.S. (*Dal Segno*) Repeat 'from the sign' 𝄋 (a decorated letter 'S')

Fine 'End'. *D.C. al Fine* means repeat 'from the beginning, then end at the word *Fine*'

Dal segno 𝄋 *al* ⊕ *e poi Coda* Repeat 'from the sign 𝄋 to ⊕, and then the Coda'

Alla ripetizione dal 𝄋 *al* ⊕ 'During the repeat, skip from the sign 𝄋 to the sign ⊕'

93

7 SIGNS, SYMBOLS AND ABBREVIATIONS

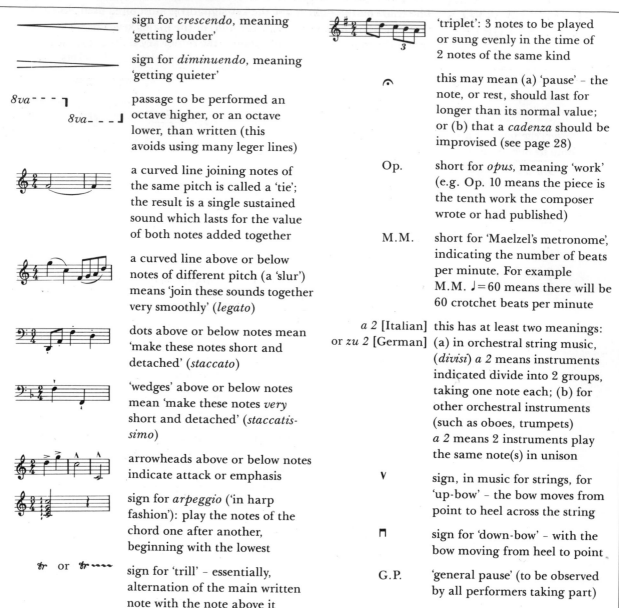

sign for *crescendo*, meaning 'getting louder'

sign for *diminuendo*, meaning 'getting quieter'

8va - - - ⌐
     8va - - - ⌐
passage to be performed an octave higher, or an octave lower, than written (this avoids using many leger lines)

a curved line joining notes of the same pitch is called a 'tie'; the result is a single sustained sound which lasts for the value of both notes added together

a curved line above or below notes of different pitch (a 'slur') means 'join these sounds together very smoothly' (*legato*)

dots above or below notes mean 'make these notes short and detached' (*staccato*)

'wedges' above or below notes mean 'make these notes *very short and detached*' (*staccatissimo*)

arrowheads above or below notes indicate attack or emphasis

sign for *arpeggio* ('in harp fashion'): play the notes of the chord one after another, beginning with the lowest

tr or *tr⌇⌇⌇*   sign for 'trill' – essentially, alternation of the main written note with the note above it

'triplet': 3 notes to be played or sung evenly in the time of 2 notes of the same kind

this may mean (a) 'pause' – the note, or rest, should last for longer than its normal value; or (b) that a *cadenza* should be improvised (see page 28)

Op. short for *opus*, meaning 'work' (e.g. Op. 10 means the piece is the tenth work the composer wrote or had published)

M.M. short for 'Maelzel's metronome', indicating the number of beats per minute. For example M.M. ♩=60 means there will be 60 crotchet beats per minute

a 2 [Italian] or *zu 2* [German] this has at least two meanings: (a) in orchestral string music, (*divisi*) *a 2* means instruments indicated divide into 2 groups, taking one note each; (b) for other orchestral instruments (such as oboes, trumpets) *a 2* means 2 instruments play the same note(s) in unison

V sign, in music for strings, for 'up-bow' – the bow moves from point to heel across the string

⊓ sign for 'down-bow' – with the bow moving from heel to point

G.P. 'general pause' (to be observed by all performers taking part)

8 TRANSPOSING INSTRUMENTS

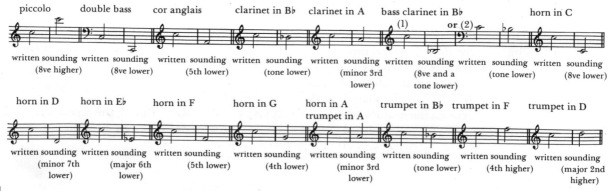

9 ABBREVIATIONS FOR REPEATED NOTES

Composers sometimes use special abbreviations to indicate notes or bars which are to be repeated – a kind of 'musical shorthand' which saves time and trouble, and also expense when the music is engraved. Here are various examples of these abbreviations showing how they are performed.

Repetition of a bar, or part of a bar, is shown by a slash, usually with a dot on each side, or by a double slash:

10 FOREIGN NAMES FOR NOTES AND KEYS

English	Italian	French	German
major	maggiore	majeur	dur
minor	minore	mineur	moll
C	do	ut	C
C sharp	do diesis	ut dièse	Cis
D flat	re bemolle	ré bémol	Des
D	re	ré	D
D sharp	re diesis	ré dièse	Dis
E flat	mi bemolle	mi bémol	Es
E	mi	mi	E
E sharp	mi diesis	mi dièse	Eis
F flat	fa bemolle	fa bémol	Fes
F	fa	fa	F
F sharp	fa diesis	fa dièse	Fis
G flat	sol bemolle	sol bémol	Ges
G	sol	sol	G
G sharp	sol diesis	sol dièse	Gis
A flat	la bemolle	la bémol	As
A	la	la	A
A sharp	la diesis	la dièse	Ais
B flat	si bemolle	si bémol	B
B	si	si	H
B sharp	si diesis	si dièse	His
C flat	do bemolle	do bémol	Ces

Notice that the German equivalent to our note B is H; and that for B flat, Germans use simply the letter B (so, for instance, *Klarinette in B* indicates 'clarinet in B *flat*').

11 ITALIAN TERMS

A Terms connected with tempo (speed, or pace)

grave, serious, grave – usually very slow
lento, slow
largo, broad, slow
larghetto, rather broadly
adagio, leisurely – usually quite slow
andante, 'easy-going', at a walking pace
andantino, slightly faster than *andante*
moderato, moderately
allegretto, not as fast as *allegro*
allegro, fast, lively
vivace, full of life
presto, very fast
prestissimo, as fast as possible

Terms marking a **change** of tempo:

accelerando [*accel.*], getting quicker
stretto or *stringendo* [*string.*], hurrying
allargando [*allarg.*], broadening
rallentando [*rall.*] ⎫ ⎧ slowing down
ritardando [*rit.*] ⎬ ⎨ gradually
ritenuto, [*rit., riten.*], held back
meno mosso, less moved, slower
più mosso, more moved, quicker
a tempo or *tempo primo*, return to the original speed

B Terms describing style, mood and expression

ad libitum [*ad lib.*], 'at pleasure', to be performed freely
agitato, agitated
animato, animated, lively
appassionato [*appass.*], passionately
arco, bowed
ben, well; *ben marcato*, well marked
cantabile [*cant.*], in a singing style
con, with (*con brio*, with vigour; *con fuoco*, with fire; *con moto*, with movement; *con spirito*, with spirit)
deciso, with decision, firmly
divisi [*div.*], divided (cancelled by *unisono* [*unis.*], in unison)
dolce [*dol.*], sweetly
doloroso, sorrowful
energico, with energy
espressivo [*esp., espress.*], expressively
giocoso, playful, humorous
giusto, just, exact (*tempo giusto*, at the exact speed; in strict time)
glissando [*gliss.*], sliding
grazioso, graceful
legato [*leg.*], smoothly
leggiero [*legg.*], lightly
maestoso, majestic

marcato [*marc.*], marked
mesto, sad
mezza voce [*m.v.*], 'half voice', half power
pesante, heavily
pizzicato [*pizz.*], plucked (cancelled by *arco*, bowed)
risoluto, resolutely
scherzando, jokingly, playfully
semplice, in a simple way
sempre, always, continually
sensibile, sensitive
senza, without
simile [*sim.*], similarly, in the same way
smorzando [*smorz.*], dying away
sordino [*sord.*], mute; *con sordini*, with mutes
sostenuto [*sost.*], sustained
sotto voce, 'under the voice', in an undertone
staccato [*stacc.*], detached, short
tacet, is silent; *tacent*, are silent
tenuto [*ten.*], held
tranquillo, tranquil, calm
tutti, everybody plays
unisono [*unis.*], in unison
vivo, lively

To many of the above terms, other words may be added such as:

assai, very
ma, but
meno, less
molto, much, very

non troppo, not too much
più, more
poco, little, rather, slightly
poco a poco, little by little

subito, suddenly
tosto, rather, somewhat